Thinking About College

PAYING FOR COLLEGE

PRACTICAL, CREATIVE STRATEGIES

Barbara Gottfried Hollander

ROSEN
PUBLISHING®

New York

This book is dedicated to my parents,
who always valued education.

Published in 2010 by The Rosen Publishing Group, Inc.
29 East 21st Street, New York, NY 10010

Copyright © 2010 by The Rosen Publishing Group, Inc.

First Edition

All rights reserved. No part of this book may be reproduced in any form without permission in writing from the publisher, except by a reviewer.

Library of Congress Cataloging-in-Publication Data

Hollander, Barbara, 1970–
Paying for college: practical, creative strategies / Barbara Gottfried Hollander. — 1st ed.
    p. cm. — (Thinking about college)
Includes bibliographical references and index.
ISBN 978-1-4358-3599-3 (library binding)
ISBN 978-1-4358-8504-2 (pbk)
ISBN 978-1-4358-8505-9 (6 pack)
1. College costs — United States. 2. Student aid — United States. 3. Education, Higher — United States — Finance. I. Title.
LB2342.H523 2010
378.3'80973 — dc22

2009018681

Manufactured in Malaysia

CPSIA Compliance Information: Batch #TWW10YA: For Further Information contact Rosen Publishing, New York, New York at 1-800-237-9932

Contents

Introduction

College may seem expensive, but the sticker price is not what most students pay for it. Would you apply to one of the best schools in the country if it cost $50,000 a year? Now what if that same school only cost you $4,000 a year? Does that sound too good to be true? In Kaplan/*Newsweek*'s *How to Get Into*

There are many ways to pay for college. With proper planning, the dream of a college education can be your reality.

College 2009, Barbara Kantrowitz reports that the sticker price of Harvard University was $48,550 for the 2007–08 academic year. However, the cost of attendance for families who earned $60,000 per year was only $4,000! How do students pay less than the sticker price for a college education? By being informed and equipped with financial strategies that lower their tuition and other costs.

A strategy is a plan to achieve a goal. In this case, you need a strategy to make college affordable for you. There are many ways to pay less than a college's "sticker price." When you are shopping for a new car, the sticker price is the full, listed price of the car, before any discounts or negotiations. A college's sticker price is the full, listed price of attending a school, before you receive any financial aid or apply any cost-cutting measures. Most students pay less—sometimes, a lot less—than the sticker price. This book will help you figure out the best strategies to lower college costs so that an affordable education can be a reality for you.

Chapter 1

What Does College Cost?

For most students, college is simply the place you go after you graduate from high school. The U.S. Bureau of Labor Statistics reports that about 69 percent of 2008 high school graduates enrolled in colleges and universities. But others may see college as too much schooling, too expensive, or too difficult. They may even prefer to get a job that pays today, rather than wait another two to four years or more to start a career and earn money. The big question facing many high school students is: Why go to college?

College: Is It Worth the Cost?

The most obvious and practical reason to go to college is money. While college does cost money, you can earn more money once you graduate. The highest-paying jobs in America, including those of doctor, dentist, and airline pilot, all require a college education. According to a 2007 study by the U.S. Census Bureau, people who have only a high school diploma earn an average of $32,500 a year. However, workers with a college degree earn an average of $53,000. Those with professional degrees beyond college, such as a degree in law or medicine, typically earn over $100,000—that's more than triple! The salary that a working person earns usually increases each

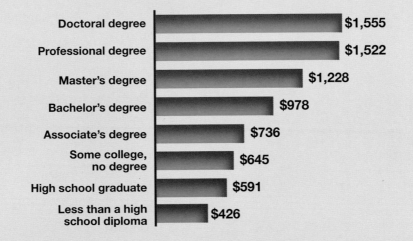

Education pays

Median weekly earnings in 2008

Education level	Median weekly earnings
Doctoral degree	$1,555
Professional degree	$1,522
Master's degree	$1,228
Bachelor's degree	$978
Associate's degree	$736
Some college, no degree	$645
High school graduate	$591
Less than a high school diploma	$426

This graph from the Bureau of Labor Statistics (http://www.bls.gov/emp/emptab7.htm) shows the average weekly earnings of Americans in 2008, for adults with different education levels. Statistics show that the more education you have, the more money you will earn. A higher salary will make your needs and wants more affordable.

year. So a college graduate who earns a larger salary in the first years of his or her career continues to earn more money than a high school graduate. In fact, the College Board reports that a college graduate earns $1 million more on average in a lifetime than a high school graduate.

A college education also gives you more job opportunities. Online job listings tell you what employers are looking for in a worker, including job skills, required level of education, and work

Two-Year Associate's Degree	Four-Year Bachelor's Degree	Graduate College
• Aircraft and Avionics Technicians	• Accountants	• Advanced-Practice Nurses
• Cardiovascular Technologists	• Air Traffic Controllers	• Archaeologists
• Computer Support Specialists	• Clinical Laboratory Technologists	• College Professors
• Dental Hygienists	• Computer Systems Analysts	• Curators
• Drafters	• Construction Managers	• Dentists
• Engineering Technicians	• Engineers	• Doctors
• Forestry Technicians	• Federal Agents	• Economists
• Human-Service Assistants	• Graphic Designers	• Lawyers
• Lodging Managers	• Insurance Agents	• Librarians
• Paralegals	• Journalists	• Physical Therapists
• Pharmacy Technicians	• Landscape Architects	• Psychologists
• Physical Therapist Assistants	• Personal Financial Advisors	• Rehabilitation Counselors
• Preschool Teachers	• Physician Assistants	• Scientists
• Registered Nurses	• Teachers	• Statisticians
• Science Technicians	• Wildlife Technicians	• Veterinarians

Different jobs require different levels of education. An engineer can work in the field after four years of college, but a lawyer requires an additional three years of graduate schooling. Source: http://www.collegeboard.com/student/csearch/majors_careers/232.html.

experience. Often, employers mention that job applicants need a B.A. degree or other degree. The abbreviation "B.A." stands for Bachelor of Arts, which is a type of undergraduate college degree. Other abbreviations, such as "M.A." (which stands for Master of

Arts), specify graduate degrees, which are obtained after you finish college and complete more schooling. In today's world, many jobs require a college or graduate degree.

Employers are now becoming more selective. Many are requiring their workers to have more qualifications, such as a college degree. Since more people are applying for fewer jobs, employers can be choosy and hire those with the most education. The recent economic recession has made the odds for job hunters even worse. One morning in February 2009, more than one thousand people lined up in Miami, Florida, to apply for only thirty-five firefighter jobs! During a recession, or economic downturn, many people lose their jobs and are looking for work. Businesses are also closing and hiring fewer workers. In a tight market, people with college degrees are more likely to get the available jobs.

A college education also provides needed skills for the workplace. Many college courses give you the opportunity to express yourself through writing, speaking, researching, analyzing, and problem-solving activities. These are skills that will help you throughout your life and career. Also, many college courses now require students to complete assignments or projects online. This strengthens skills frequently used in today's workplace: more than half of the workers in the United States use computers daily for Internet use, messaging, word processing, managing information, and keeping track of schedules. Studies have also shown that college-educated adults are happier, healthier people who are more likely to give back to their communities through service, leadership, and charitable giving, when compared to their high school counterparts.

College increases your understanding of the world and those who live in it. There are so many things to learn in college, and what you study is your choice. In fact, there are more

According to a 2009 report by Public Agenda and the National Center for Public Policy and Higher Education, 55 percent of adults surveyed believe that a college education is needed to be successful.

than nine hundred different majors! You can learn about various cultures, acquire more skills for the jobs that you want, and even participate in programs around the world. There are many college counselors and tutoring services available to help you succeed. So academic subjects that were difficult for you in high school may seem easier or more enjoyable in college.

College is an investment in you. It provides new and exciting opportunities, especially for students who are the first in their families to go to college. With a bit of effort and research, higher education is available to everyone. In 2007, 20 percent of college students came from families who earned less than $20,000 a year. Kathleen Blanco, the first woman governor of Louisiana, once said, "Almost every educated person has a job and a way out of poverty." College is your choice for better work, more money, and a brighter future.

Overcoming Sticker Shock

College is expensive. According to the College Board, a four-year public college in 2008–09 cost an average of $6,585 per year in tuition and fees alone. Tuition and fees at a two-year public college cost an average of $2,402 per year. It's true that some private colleges cost $35,000 a year or more. Do not let these costs scare you. Most students pay less than the sticker price.

When you research colleges online or in books, there is an "annual cost" section with the most recent sticker prices. For example, the College Handbook published by the College Board lists the annual costs of 3,800 four-year colleges and two-year colleges and technical schools. These costs often include tuition and fees, and estimates for books, supplies, and personal expenses. If you are interested in a particular college, you can also look at the college's Web site for tuition information.

The College Board reports that room and board in 2008–09 cost an average of $7,748 per year for a public four-year college and $8,989 for a private four-year college.

Understanding Cost Factors

When trying to estimate the total cost of college, the numbers can be confusing. There are direct costs, including tuition

and room and board, which are paid directly to the college. There are also indirect costs associated with going to college. This category includes books and supplies, transportation, and personal expenses. The term "cost of attendance," or COA, includes both direct and indirect costs.

Direct Costs

Tuition refers to the actual cost of attending college classes. It can be calculated by the number of credits you take (each class is assigned a number of credits), or by your status as either a part-time or full-time student. For public colleges, the price you're charged for tuition often depends on whether you are a state resident or not. For example, in 2008–09, Nassau Community College in Garden City, New York, charged $1,776 in tuition for a full-time, in-state student, but $3,552 for a full-time, out-of-state student. Many colleges also charge additional fees, such as fees for student activities and health insurance.

Students who choose to live on campus pay for room and board. "Room" refers to the amount that you pay for a dormitory

Good Choices Can Lower College Costs

- **Factor in Location.** When applying to colleges, think of the costs of the location. For example, rent and food are more expensive in New York City than in Rockford, Illinois.

- **Share your Living expenses.** Get a roommate. Roommates share living expenses, including rent, utilities, and food. For example, if your rent is $600 a month and you have a roommate, each of you pays only $300 a month.

- **Work in the dormitory.** If you want to live in the dormitories, consider being a resident advisor (RA). The RA receives lower room and board fees or tuition because he or she works in the dorm, usually taking care of the students on his or her floor. The RA may also receive other financial benefits, such as a meal plan, an allowance for laundry services, a fitness center membership, or small cash stipends.

- **Consider Living at home.** According to the Web site of Senator Barbara Boxer of California (http://boxer.senate.gov/students/collegeprep/financial/reducingcosts.cfm), students who live at home and commute to college can save up to $6,000 each year.

- **Cut transportation costs.** Consider taking public transportation or carpooling, rather than driving. These options are better for the environment and your wallet.

- **Research your meal options.** If you choose a college meal plan, research your options. For example, some plans require you to pay for a certain number of meals, no matter what you decide to eat at each meal. Going "a la carte" means only paying for what you do eat. If you have an apartment and buy your own food, be a wise shopper. Look for sales and clip coupons. Don't eat out often—it can quickly add up.

- **Find used books or download.** Books and supplies averaged $1,000 in 2008–09, says the College Board. To save money, find used books online. You can buy used textbooks at sites such as http://www.textbookx.com and swap fiction and literature at sites such as http://www.paperbackswap.com. Some college bookstores sell used books and buy back books at the end of the semester. Download textbooks for free at such sites as http://www.textbookrevolution.org and http://www.opentextbook.org. Also, borrow books you need from local libraries or rent them at http://www.chegg.com.

- **Look for computer deals.** Apple, Microsoft, and many colleges offer student discounts. Some college computer labs even give out free software at the start of the school year.

- **Reduce your number of credits.** Students who score well on certain exams, such as Advanced Placement and CLEP tests, can receive college credit at many schools. This lowers the total number of billable credits needed to graduate.

room to live in for the school year. This amount may also include electricity, phone service, and Internet access. "Board" is the amount that you pay for food. Colleges offer different meal plans that may include both on- and off-campus options.

Indirect Costs

Indirect costs are sometimes called variable costs because they can vary from person to person and from semester to semester. Transportation is an example of a variable cost. For those living at home, there will be commuting costs associated with getting to and from college. You may take the bus, train, subway, or your own car. For those living on campus, there will be traveling expenses for your initial trip to college, for your trip home when the school year ends, and for midyear visits (for example, during the holidays).

Indirect costs include buying books for classes and paying fees for lab materials, if you are taking science courses that require labs. You will also need basic supplies, such as paper and pencils, and you may choose more expensive items like a laptop computer. Personal expenses, such as food outside the cafeteria, personal items, clothing, entertainment, and outside health insurance plans, are also indirect costs. Try to realistically budget these expenses—they are good places to cut costs.

Preparing for Rising Costs

Have you ever heard an older person say, "When I was your age, milk only cost 25 cents a carton?" It's true that average prices of goods and services rise each year. This rise in the general price level is called inflation. College tuition also suffers from inflation. According to Peterson's *Paying for College*, tuition costs rise at a rate of about 6 percent per year. The

Careful budgeting of variable costs, such as food, books, and school supplies, can reduce your college expenses.

loan industry that helps students pay for college has also grown at a rate of 27 percent between 2002 and 2007.

To calculate your college costs, you should factor in inflation. To do this, you will need to know the inflation factor. This is the number by which you multiply the present cost in order to determine your inflation-adjusted cost. According to the current national average, the cost of college is increasing at a rate of about 6 percent a year. Therefore, if you are planning to begin college a year from now, take the current cost of college and multiply it by 1.06 to find the likely cost of your first year. For example, if the yearly total cost (tuition, housing, food, and other expenses) for a college is $10,000 today, your annual total cost will be about $10,600 when you begin college in one year. If you are beginning college in two years, your inflation factor is 1.12. For each year, the factor increases by about .06. There are free online computer programs that figure out college costs with inflation for you, such as Sallie Mae's Education Investment Planner at http://www.salliemae.com.

There are some ways for families to pay for college without worrying about rising costs. For example, in some states the 529 prepaid tuition plan allows people to buy college credits at today's prices. So even if inflation makes college more expensive next year, you are still paying today's college costs. Who pays the difference? The state government pays the extra money as long as you attend an in-state public college. Some states allow students to transfer the amount that the state pays to private or out-of-state colleges. However, in these cases, students may not receive the full value of their contribution. Some colleges now offer their own 529 prepaid tuition plans.

College Savings Plans

The 529 savings plan, which is different from the 529 prepaid tuition plan, allows families to put money into a special account that they will use to pay for college. State governments run the plan. Find your state's plan at http://www.savingforcollege.com. You can apply to 529 plans in other states, too. You can open an account with $250 and then deposit $50 or more each month. The federal government will not tax any money taken out to pay for college. Your account balance grows in interest, which is also not taxed by the federal government.

The Coverdell Education Savings Account (ESA) is another way to save for college. This account allows parents to put in up to $2,000 each year to pay for their children's education.

Money can be directly deposited into a savings account for college. Accounts that offer the highest interest rates will earn you the most money on your balance. Use an online tuition savings calculator to figure out the yearly deposits needed to cover your educational costs.

Interest earned is tax-free. The money you withdraw to pay for college is not taxed as long as it does not exceed the cost of your education. Ask your parents, grandparents, aunts, and uncles to invest in a college savings plan for you.

Through his administration's policies, President Barack Obama aims to make college more affordable for millions of students.

Hope Scholarship Tax Credit/ American Opportunity Tax Credit

A tax credit is another way that the government helps parents who want to send their children to college. The Hope Scholarship is a need-based tax credit. In the past, it gave parents up to $1,650 in tax breaks when they spent at least $2,200 of their own money to pay for college, including tuition and course materials. In 2009, President Barack Obama created a newer version called the American Opportunity Tax Credit. It raised the tax-break limit to $2,500 when parents spend $4,000 on college—that is an extra $850 for each student who qualifies! These changes were aimed at helping students in low-income and middle-income families pay for college so that attaining a higher education and a high-paying job can be a reality for everyone. The tax credit is available to students in their first and second years of college, for every child in the family.

What can this mean for you? The College Board reports that the average community college cost $2,402 in tuition and fees in 2008–09. If you receive an American Opportunity Tax Credit, your tuition and fees might be paid! Now, think about your other college costs. Room and board can be expensive, but not if you live at home or find an inexpensive apartment and get some roommates. Finally, many college Web sites estimate the cost of books and supplies to be about $1,000 for an academic year. Guess what? The new American Opportunity Tax Credit pays for course materials, too. Your college education just became more affordable.

Choosing a College That You Can Afford

It's important for you to understand that there are many types of colleges available to you. Different types of colleges mean different costs.

Four-Year Colleges

There are more than two thousand four-year colleges in the United States. These colleges offer many programs for high school graduates that require an average of four years to complete. After finishing a four-year program, students usually receive either a Bachelor of Arts (B.A.) degree or Bachelor of Science (B.S.) degree. Students pay tuition and fees to attend these colleges. But the four-year college you choose determines how much you will pay.

Public vs. Private Colleges

During the 2008–09 academic year, if a student from New York decided to attend the University at Buffalo full-time, he or she faced a sticker price of over $6,000 in tuition and fees. However, if that same student planned to attend New York University, he or she faced a sticker price of over $37,000 in tuition and fees. That is more than a $30,000 difference for one year!

Why is tuition so much more at New York University? The main reason is that NYU is a private

Prospective students and their families tour the campus of the University of California, Berkeley, a public university. More than 220,000 students attend college on one of the ten campuses of the University of California system.

university, but the University at Buffalo is a public university. Four-year colleges can be public, private, or for-profit institutions. In 2007, about 78 percent of the 15.4 million college students in the United States attended public colleges and universities.

Public colleges, like public elementary, middle, and high schools, receive money from their state governments. This money is spent on the expenses of the colleges, such as paying the professors' salaries, maintaining campus buildings, and buying uniforms for the athletic teams. Private universities also have these expenses, but they either do not receive money from the state or they receive less than the public colleges. They also tend to spend more money per student on academic resources and campus facilities. So they charge higher tuitions in order to get the money they need. In addition, private schools often have higher room and board fees than public colleges. So going to a public college or university can save you money.

On the other hand, even if your family is not wealthy, don't rule out attending a private college. Some private colleges— such as Cooper Union and Olin College of Engineering—are tuition-free or have deeply reduced tuitions. Also, some private schools with high sticker prices have begun to offer substantial financial aid packages, making them as affordable, or even more affordable, than public schools.

According to CNBC, "Since December 2007, seven of the eight Ivy League universities have announced major overhauls to their financial aid offerings, which in most cases substantially increases aid for low- and middle-income families."

Harvard was the first to change its financial aid structure, by replacing loans with grants and instituting the "Zero to 10 Percent Standard." According to this rule, low- and middle-income families are expected to pay no more than 10 percent of their annual income for Harvard. In some income categories, families are expected to contribute zero.

Working Part-Time Can Help Pay for College

Students can reasonably earn between $2,000 and $4,000 in a year while going to school, as well as extra money in the summer. Considering that the average cost of community college was $2,402 in 2008–09, working can pay your college tuition! According to the August 2008 NextPath newsletter, the top-paying part-time jobs for college students include computer lab assistant or computer support specialist, administrative assistant, aerobics instructor or fitness trainer, library assistant, bank teller, hotel desk clerk, and babysitter. Some companies also offer many college students part-time work. For example, 60 percent of the part-time employees at UPS are college students.

Wages can range from $8 per hour to approximately $22 per hour in many of these popular jobs. To calculate your gross weekly pay, multiply the number of hours you plan to work in a week by the hourly wage. For example, if you plan to work ten hours a week in a job that pays $10 per hour, then your gross pay would be $100 per week. And, if you worked for nine months, or thirty-six weeks, then you would make $3,600 during the school year. Remember that your gross pay is higher than the amount you will actually receive, because it does not include items, such as taxes, that are subtracted from your paycheck.

Therefore, when applying to colleges, do not be overly discouraged by sticker prices. You may end up paying less at a more expensive, private college because of the school's financial aid offer.

In-State vs. Out-of-State

A public college is less expensive than a private college because it receives money from the state government. This money comes from taxes paid by the people living in the state. The taxpayers can then choose to send their children to a state school, if they are accepted, and benefit from the lower cost of tuition. But what if a person living in Maryland wants to attend a Michigan state school, such as the University of Michigan? Does the student from Maryland pay the same tuition as a student from Michigan? No.

The students pay different tuitions to attend the same school. The family of the Michigan student has been paying taxes to Michigan's state government, and the state government has been giving some of this money to the state's colleges. However, the family of the Maryland student has not been paying Michigan taxes, so they must pay more in tuition to attend a state school in Michigan.

In fact, in 2008–09, a freshman student from the state of Michigan (also known as a "resident") faced a sticker price of $10,848 in tuition and fees to attend the University of Michigan at Ann Arbor. But a student from any other state (an "out-of-state resident") faced a sticker price of $32,880 in tuition and fees. The same school had a $22,000 difference in the sticker price! Not all in-state and out-of-state tuitions have that large a difference, but public universities do charge in-state students less in tuition. So going to a state college in your home state can save you money.

Full-Time vs. Part-Time Students

Student status is another factor that determines college costs. If you are a full-time student, you must take a certain number of credits per semester, as determined by the college. You can also choose to be a part-time student and take fewer credits.

Many students work part-time to pay for college. In fact, the American Council on Education reports that nearly 80 percent of undergraduate students work while pursuing a college education and that the majority of these students are employed off campus.

Many students in two-year colleges are part-time students who also have paying jobs while they attend school. Descriptions of two-year colleges, also called their profiles, often tell you what percentage of students goes to school part-time.

Two-Year Colleges

Another type of college is a two-year or community college. Almost half the college students in the United States attend community colleges. These colleges offer degrees to students who often live at home. Students who complete a two-year program typically earn an associate's degree.

Two-year colleges can train students in a particular area, such as business, computers, early childhood education, graphic design, and social services. Also, they usually provide students with more academic help. Many of these colleges have articulation agreements with four-year colleges. This means the credit received from a two-year college can be transferred to a four-year college, as long as the credits are in areas the four-year school requires for graduation. This is important because a student who graduates from a two-year college and then transfers successfully to a four-year one will only need two more years to earn a bachelor's degree.

The two-year college option saves students a lot of money, since two-year colleges have lower tuitions. Here is a list of the College Board's average tuition and fees for 2008–09:

- Two-Year College: $2,402
- In-State, Four-Year Public College: $6,585
- Out-Of-State, Four-Year College: $17,452
- Four-Year Private College or University: $25,143

Students gather near the admissions department at Prince George's Community College in Largo, Maryland. According to the American Association of Community Colleges, 11.5 million students attend community colleges, and 39 percent of these students are the "first generation to attend college."

With these prices, if you decided to attend a two-year college and then transfer to a four-year public college, your tuition and fees would cost about $8,400 less than if you attended a four-year public college for all four years! So, as long as you take enough courses toward your eventual major and other requirements, attending a two-year college can save you money on a four-year program.

Calculating the Cost of Attendance

Making a cost-of-attendance (COA) worksheet will give you an idea of what a college will cost. This worksheet is based on estimates for both direct and indirect costs. Today, there are many computer programs that will help you figure out the COA for colleges you're interested in.

For example, the Web site of the student loan company Sallie Mae, http://www.salliemae.com, has a tool called the Education Investment Planner. You can use this online tool to research the cost of more than 5,500 schools. Once you enter information about yourself and the name of the college or university, the planner projects, or forecasts, your cost per year to attend that school, taking into account rising prices.

To begin your search, select the status of "student." Then provide your student information:

- Your school year (for example, "junior in high school")
- Type of degree you want to get (such as "bachelor's degree" for a four-year college or "associate's degree" for a two-year college)
- Name of the state where you live
- Whether or not you are a U.S. citizen

Also, you will need to check off where you are in the application process. For example, if you are just looking, select "Researching schools but haven't applied yet."

The next screen, "Estimating Costs," asks you about the type of college you are interested in. If you're researching a particular school, type in its name. If you are not sure, choose a school type like a four-year public college. Then choose a possible location and indicate whether that makes you an in-state student or an out-of-state student. The program also asks when you plan to start, how many years you plan to attend, and what your enrollment status will be (part-time or full-time).

Finally, Sallie Mae's Education Investment Planner will give you an estimate of the cost of your college education for one year. The planner breaks down the cost into several categories, including tuition and fees, room and board, and books and supplies. (You need to do your own thinking about the probable cost of your personal expenses, transportation, etc.) It can also give you estimates for the increases in college costs over the next few years. Remember that the answers you enter—and the program's results—are only best guesses. Try putting in different answers to compare your options. For example, try the planner with a four-year public college and again with a community college. Or compare your cost of attending a public college with the cost of attending a private one.

It's important to remember that the cost the program gives you is not necessarily the amount you will pay. These estimates don't take into account the financial aid you may receive, such as loans and scholarships. According to David Rye in *The Complete Idiot's Guide to Financial Aid for College*, 55 percent of students received financial aid in 2008. The next chapter talks about the money that is available to help you pay for college.

What Is Financial Aid?

Chapter 3

Financial aid is money given by the government, colleges, businesses, and organizations to help students pay for college. It allows them to pay less than the sticker price for a higher education. More than $143 billion in financial aid was available to undergraduate and graduate students in 2008 and 2009, according to the College Board.

There are two main types of financial aid: loans, and gifts in the form of grants and scholarships. Loans, which must be repaid, make up the largest portion of financial aid. Grants and scholarships provide students with "free money" that doesn't have to be paid back. In addition, work-study programs are a common element in many students' financial aid packages. Work-study programs require students to work part-time to help pay for school.

Where the Money Comes From

Most of the money for financial aid comes from the federal and state governments. According to Sallie Mae, more than half the government aid given out in 2007–08 came from the federal government. There is also institutional aid. Institutional aid is money given to students by colleges and universities. Sallie Mae reported that 21 percent of financial aid came from educational institutions in 2007–08. Other sources, such as private grants and tuition assistance programs from parents' employers, made up 7 percent

A campus visit should include a trip to the financial aid office.

of financial aid for that year. Ask your parents if the organizations where they work have tuition plans.

Who Can Apply

All students can apply for financial aid. They can even apply at different times, including while in high school, college, or graduate school. Financial aid is divided into two categories: non-need-based and need-based aid. Non-need-based aid does not depend on your family's financial status. Instead, it may be given to students who do well in areas like academics or sports, or who have a certain background or interest. Non-need-based aid is also called merit-based aid.

Talented scholar-athletes may be able to win athletic scholarships or academic and community scholarships. Such scholarships are examples of merit-based aid.

Need-based aid depends on your family's financial status, such as how much your parents earn from working and the value of their home or other property. When deciding on need-based aid, families are put into three categories: low income (families who earn less than $25,000 a year), middle income (families who earn between $25,000 and $70,000 a year), and high income (families who earn more than $70,000 a year). The less money your family has to pay for college, the more need-based aid you can receive.

Free Application for Federal Student Aid (FAFSA)

To apply for need-based aid, you have to fill out a Free Application for Federal Student Aid (FAFSA). You can pick up an application at your high school or college financial aid office. You can also fill it out online (in English or Spanish) at http://www.fafsa.ed.gov. You fill out the FAFSA once to apply for all kinds of financial aid for the upcoming school year. Then you will need to renew it each year. Filling out financial aid forms can be intimidating. But remember that the reward for completing the FAFSA could be thousands of dollars for your college education.

Eighty percent of students choose to fill out the FAFSA online. To apply online, you need a personal identification number (PIN). Choose a number that you will remember because you will need it whenever you want to change or renew your FAFSA. The first page of the FAFSA Web site tells you the deadlines for each state. Even if you live in a state with a July deadline, it is still best to apply as early as you can (in January, if possible). More money is given out early in the year.

The FAFSA site lists what you will need to fill out the form, including your Social Security number, your parents' Social Security numbers, your driver's license number (if you have one), and your alien registration number (if you are not a U.S. citizen). You will also need current federal tax information for you and your parents, any untaxed income information like welfare benefits, and information on assets (items with financial value that you own, including savings). This may seem like a lot of information, but if you have your parents' current tax returns, you have most of the information already.

The FAFSA has four sections: Student Information, Student Dependency Status, Parental Information, and Student Finances. There is also a worksheet at the end of the application

A parent, guidance counselor, or financial aid officer can help you obtain and complete financial aid forms.

to help you figure out the numbers. Finally, as part of your application, you will list your college choices by their codes. The colleges that you choose will have access to your FAFSA results and will use this information to put together your financial aid offers. It is important to include all of the colleges that you are interested in. You can also add and delete colleges throughout the process. After you complete the FAFSA, check it over. Then submit your application. Within three weeks, you should receive a Student Aid Report (SAR). If you don't receive this form, find out why by contacting the Federal Student Aid Program.

The Student Aid Report summarizes your FAFSA information and informs you of your expected family contribution (EFC). The EFC is the amount your family is expected to pay for college. The cost of attendance minus your expected family contribution equals the financial aid that you need. This aid can come from a combination of loans, scholarships and grants, and work-study programs. Even if your SAR says you are not eligible to receive federal need-based aid, you can still apply for merit-based grants and scholarships. Also, a student who does not receive financial aid from the federal government can still receive need-based aid from his or her state government. So apply and don't give up!

College Scholarship Service (CSS)/ Financial Aid PROFILE

Some colleges and scholarship programs require students to complete the CSS/Financial Aid PROFILE. According to the College Board, which provides this application, about 600 colleges use the profile to make decisions about who receives nonfederal financial aid (private grants and scholarships). The CSS asks for more detailed information than the FAFSA, and must be completed before the FAFSA is filled out. If your college requires this form, you can obtain it at https://profileonline.collegeboard.com. Filling out the CSS is not free. It requires an application fee of $25 and an additional fee of $16 per college or scholarship program. Students from low-income families who are registering for the CSS/Financial Aid PROFILE services for the first time may not have to pay some of these fees.

Your Financial Aid Package

Your EFC is given to all of the colleges that you listed on your FAFSA. These colleges will use this number to determine your financial aid packages. Remember to fill out your college applications as early as possible. Colleges are more likely to give financial aid to a student who has already been accepted to the school.

Next, your college choices will send you financial aid offers. An offer lists your estimated expenses (such as tuition, room and board, and books) and the financial aid that will help you meet these costs. The package will probably include all three types of aid. Look at the breakdown of the financial aid. How much of it is in the form of grants and scholarships (money that doesn't need to be repaid) versus loans (money that must be repaid)? Which types are renewable (meaning you

Meet with a financial aid officer at your chosen college to get information you need about applying for financial aid.

must reapply to receive them for next year)? Remember that the FAFSA needs to be resubmitted annually, in order for you to continue to receive financial aid. Also, many scholarships require you to reapply each year and show that you are keeping your grades up.

When you receive all your financial aid packages, compare them. Which college gives the best package? Compare the types of aid given, especially loans versus grants. While loans can be helpful, money given outright is more valuable than loans.

Remember to sign, date, and send back the offers from the colleges you are considering. Don't let a school give away your aid because you returned your offer letter too late. Also, be sure to pay attention to other forms that a college's financial aid office may ask you to complete, including verification forms that ask you to verify, or confirm, your information.

If your family's contribution and the financial aid package still don't cover the cost of college, you have options. First, make sure the information on your SAR is correct. Second, contact the financial aid office at your first-choice college to set up an appointment. Bring a parent if possible. Tell the counselor how interested you are in the school, and inform the counselor if you received packages from other schools with more aid. Also mention anything that happened since you filled out your FAFSA, such as a parent losing a job, which may affect the amount of money you need. Many parents and their children appeal a school's financial aid decision in order to receive more aid.

Getting Help

There are many professionals who can help you understand the world of financial aid. A high school guidance counselor can tell you about financial aid options and provide application forms. Also ask your guidance counselor for information on special programs to help high school students realize the dream of a college education. For example, Upward Bound, a program of the U.S. Department of Education, provides help for students from low-income families who will be first-generation college students (this means that neither parent has a college degree).

Beware of Financial Aid Consulting Scams

There are many reported incidents of financial aid consulting scams. People running these scams often post ads that use the word "guaranteed"—for example, "guaranteed money" or "results guaranteed." They may claim to have special connections to colleges, know things that other consultants do not, tell you to put false information on financial aid forms, or ask to be paid in full for their services right away. If you are worried about a potential financial aid scam, check out the consultant by calling the U.S. Department of Education Inspector General's hotline at (800) 647-8733. If you want to report a financial aid scam, call the Better Business Bureau at (703) 276-0100.

The help includes figuring out college plans and financial aid, SAT registration, academic support, and learning about career choices. Some programs serve only students in particular cities or school districts. Ask your counselor if there are any programs designed for students in your area.

Colleges also hire their own professionals, called financial aid officers (FAOs) or financial aid administrators (FAAs), to help students figure out ways to pay for college. If you already have a list of possible colleges, talk to the financial aid officers at those schools. Find out how they can help you afford college costs. Remember, colleges vary in the amount of money and resources available for student aid. So different colleges will be able to help you in different ways. The advice that one college's FAO gives you does not necessarily apply to another college. Speak to the FAOs at your college choices to get the most recent information.

In addition to school professionals who provide free advice, there are financial aid consultants who charge you for their services. Their fees can range from $125 an hour to package deals starting at $500. Financial aid consultants guide families through the financial aid process, from filling out applications to getting the best financial aid offers. These consultants are trained to understand financial aid and the changes in financial aid policies that may affect you. Some consultants are accountants or people who have worked for college financial aid offices in the past. Financial aid consulting services can help you, but they cost money.

With some work, you can figure out the financial aid process on your own for free. Online resources and books provide recent and important information. Most students have access to a computer at school or the local public library. Some students may also have computers at home. Many government agencies and private organizations have made understanding and applying for financial aid easier by explaining it online in English and in Spanish. Schools and public libraries have books on applying for financial aid, as well as books about available loans, scholarships, and grants. The most recent books will be found in the libraries' reference sections. Ask your librarian to help you find them.

Financial Aid During a Recession

By now, you understand that financial aid helps pay for college. There are several different types of financial aid, and anyone can apply for them. There are also many resources, including books, Web sites, and professionals, that can help you learn about and apply for financial aid. In addition, there have been changes in the financial aid industry because of the recent recession. Recessions tend to have three main effects on colleges and their costs:

1. More people apply to colleges or return to graduate schools. During a recession, many people lose their jobs, and it's harder for them to find new ones. So they go to college to learn new skills that they hope will give them more job opportunities. Remember that college helps you gain skills that are needed to find jobs. It will also give you an advantage over those who don't have a college degree.

Recession Reality Check: Forbes.com listed the ten most recession-proof jobs, which are jobs that people tend to find and keep, even in a bad economy. These jobs were in technology (computer fields), business, and nursing—all fields that require a college degree.

2. The cost of college may increase more than expected. During a recession, both public and private colleges receive less money from the government, private donations, and their own investments. Since colleges still have to pay their bills, they increase their tuitions. Such increases help pay for their expenses.

Recession Reality Check: In 2008–09, tuitions increased more than expected, and many college students had trouble meeting their college costs. But in February 2009, President Barack Obama designed an economic recovery plan that included making college more affordable for seven million students.

3. The amount of financial aid available to students usually decreases, while the amount of students applying for financial

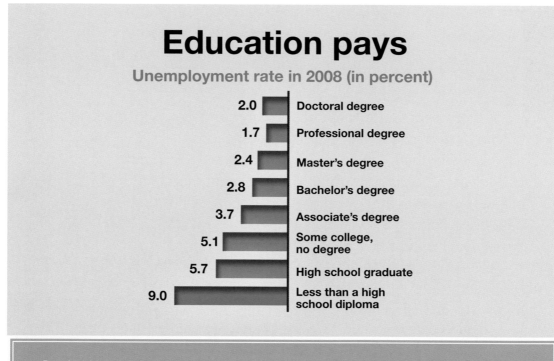

Education pays

Unemployment rate in 2008 (in percent)

2.0 Doctoral degree

1.7 Professional degree

2.4 Master's degree

2.8 Bachelor's degree

3.7 Associate's degree

5.1 Some college, no degree

5.7 High school graduate

9.0 Less than a high school diploma

People with only a high school diploma or less had the highest unemployment rates in 2008, while people with professional degrees had the lowest unemployment rate.

aid increases. Colleges are receiving less money and therefore have less money to give out as financial aid. Parents, especially those who have lost their jobs, have less money to pay for their children's college educations.

Recession Reality Check: According to *U.S. News & World Report*, there were 1.4 million more students completing the FAFSA for financial aid in 2008 than in 2007.

A recession can make paying for college more difficult. However, it also shows you how important it is to go to college so that you can get a job and keep it. As President Obama once said, "Every American needs more than a high school diploma."

Ten Great Questions
TO ASK A COLLEGE FINANCIAL AID OFFICER

1   What is the total cost of attendance for the current school year?

2   What percentage of first-year students receive financial aid?

3   How much is your tuition expected to increase in the next year?

4   How do you figure out how much financial aid a student receives?

5   Do I need to renew my financial aid package each year?

6   When are the school's deadlines for financial aid?

7   Do you meet 100 percent of your students' financial aid needs? (Need is the difference between the school's cost of attendance and the expected family contribution.)

8   What percentage of your financial aid is grants and scholarships versus loans?

9   What is the least number of credits that I need to take to keep the grants in my financial aid package?

10 Do you provide financial aid for summer school? If yes, will this impact my financial aid for the regular academic year?

Chapter 4

Loans and Work-Study Programs

An educational loan is money that you borrow to pay for school, with a promise to pay it back according to certain conditions. Most financial aid given to college students consists of loans. Education loans are given at relatively low interest rates and can be paid back in different ways over a period of time. Loans are "self-help" aid and can either be need-based or non-need-based.

Popular Types of Loans

College loans are either subsidized or unsubsidized. Subsidized loans are a good deal for students because the government pays the interest while you are in school. With unsubsidized loans, you pay the interest. Since the interest rate determines the cost of borrowing money, the lower the rate, the better.

Federal Perkins Loans

Colleges give out Perkins loans to students who show great financial need. In other words, their families cannot contribute much, if anything, to their college costs. You can receive up to $20,000 in Perkins loans during your college years. These loans are subsidized, so the government makes the interest payments. There are no loan fees, there is a nine-month grace period, and you can repay the loans over ten years.

Federal Stafford Loans

The government gives out both subsidized and unsubsidized Stafford loans. Subsidized Stafford loans are need-based, and the government pays the interest while you are attending college. With unsubsidized Stafford loans, you pay the interest. But you also have the option of paying off all the interest in one amount after you graduate. To qualify for a Stafford loan, you can be either a part-time or full-time student and can receive up to $23,000. Repayment of the loan begins six months after you finish school.

Federal Parent Loan for Undergraduate Students (PLUS) Loans

PLUS loans allow parents to borrow up to the amount that is not covered by other financial aid sources. The payments begin only sixty days after the loan has been taken out, and interest rates are generally higher than unsubsidized Stafford loans. PLUS loans don't have grace periods and do have some extra fees. The Federal PLUS loan is a Federal Family Education loan. There is also a Direct PLUS loan, given out by the Direct Loan Servicing Center. This loan is similar to the Federal PLUS loans, but may offer different interest rates. Compare the rates to get the least expensive loan.

Taking Out College Loans

To apply for all loans, you need to fill out the FAFSA, which is available online in English and Spanish. Even if you qualify for a

Financial aid officers can help you understand the terms of your loans.

loan, you can't get one if you don't apply. Some loans, such as the Stafford loans, have other forms, too. Ask your high school guidance counselor or college financial aid officer for the right forms.

Accepting a Loan

When you receive a loan offer, make sure you understand everything—especially the repayment terms. Sit down with your college's FAO (it's free), and ask him or her to go over the loan papers with you. Do you know how much you have to pay back? Are you paying the interest, or is the government paying it for you?

Ten Key Loan Terms

1. **consolidation** Taking several loans and putting them together into one loan balance.
2. **grace period** The time between graduation and the date the student is expected to begin repaying the loan.
3. **interest** The cost of borrowing money, expressed as a percentage of the loan amount.
4. **loan default** Failure to repay the loan.
5. **loan deferment** An arrangement that allows the loan amount to be repaid at a later date. The government pays the interest payments on subsidized loans for a set time.
6. **loan fees** Extra costs associated with taking out a loan, including administration and application fees.
7. **loan forgiveness** Canceling part of an education loan because the student has met specific requirements.
8. **forbearance** A postponement or reduction of loan payments for a specified time. Interest still accrues during this period.
9. **monthly payment** The amount of money that the student is expected to pay each month.
10. **repayment terms** The ways in which the student has agreed to repay the loan, including how many years the student will take to repay and when the student will be expected to start paying.

When do you start paying back the loan? Are there extra fees? What are your options for deferring your loan payments? What happens if you default?

If you accept the loan, you will receive money to pay for college. The money will either be sent in installments electronically or sent by check directly to the college. If your Perkins loan, Stafford loan, or PLUS loan is paid electronically, you or your parents will receive a letter each time a payment is made.

Repaying the Loan

Loans provide you with borrowed money that you are legally obligated to pay back. How you repay a loan depends on the loan. PLUS loans are paid back while you are still in school. But loans like the Perkins and Stafford loans are repaid after you stop going to school.

There are several ways to pay back a loan. If you have a standard repayment schedule, you will pay the same amount each month. A graduated repayment schedule lets you pay less when you first start paying back the loan and pay larger amounts later. A contingent repayment schedule bases your monthly payments on how much money you are making after you graduate. There is even an extended repayment schedule that allows you to pay back your loans over twenty-five years, if you qualify. The average college student who took out loans in 2008 will graduate with a repayment commitment of $250 each month for ten years. There are many ways to repay loans. Find a plan that works for you.

Defaulting on a Loan

Defaulting on a loan means you failed to pay it back. If you miss one loan payment, you don't default on your loan. However, this

Students should fully understand the repayment terms of their educational loans, including the monthly payment amounts and when they will be expected to start paying. Paying on time is important for keeping a high credit rating.

missed payment will show up on your credit record (a good credit record helps you buy things, such as a house or car). Before defaulting, you can ask for a forbearance, which allows you to stop making payments for a certain period of time or lower the amount you pay. Forbearances are given under certain conditions, such as having loan payments that are more than 20 percent of your income or having a national service job.

If you default on a loan, it will hurt your credit. There may be other consequences, too. If you have a job, you may be forced to use your paycheck to pay for the loan. You can also be sued for the money. However, if you find a repayment plan that works for you and make your monthly payments on time, you will build a good credit history. This will help you buy the things you want or need in the future.

Loan Forgiveness

There are certain situations where loans are forgiven, or cancelled. This means you don't need to repay them. People who receive loan forgiveness often do volunteer, medical, teaching, or public service work. They may also serve in the military.

Popular Loan Forgiveness Programs

AmeriCorps and the Peace Corps are volunteer organizations that give participants education grants, loan forgiveness, and other

Certain jobs and professions, such as teaching in low-income or high-need areas, have programs that cancel a portion of your loan.

benefits. Up to fifty thousand students participate in AmeriCorps each year, doing such jobs as building houses, carrying out health screenings, and teaching. After completing a term of service, participants are eligible for a Segal AmeriCorps Education Award to pay for tuition or to repay student loans. After a year of full-time service, or 1,700 hours, students receive a grant of $4,725; smaller amounts are awarded for part-time service. Some colleges help out more by matching these grants or by giving school credit. In addition, full-time work with AmeriCorps or the Peace Corps counts as public service work for the Public Service Loan Forgiveness Program created by Congress in 2007. For more information on AmeriCorps, visit http://www.americorps.org.

The Peace Corps gives students the chance to volunteer around the world while paying off their college loans. Participants can travel, learn about other cultures, and help people. Peace Corps volunteers can apply to defer their Stafford and Perkins loans and even cancel part of their Perkins loans. (The more years you volunteer, the more loan money is forgiven.) To learn about the Peace Corps, visit http://www.peacecorps.gov. Its Web site can even match you up with a volunteer working in another country who will answer your questions.

Loan Forgiveness Jobs

Teaching is a job that can grant you loan forgiveness. A student teaching in a low-income area can apply to have some of his or her Perkins and Stafford loans cancelled. For more information, visit http://www.federalstudentaid.ed.gov and search for "Cancellation/Deferment Options for Teachers." Teach for America, part of AmeriCorps, can also give you up

Tips for Reducing Your Loan

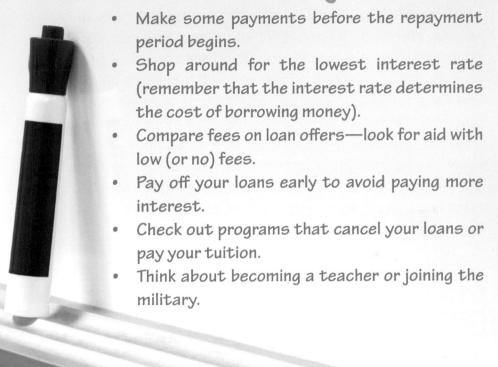

- Make some payments before the repayment period begins.
- Shop around for the lowest interest rate (remember that the interest rate determines the cost of borrowing money).
- Compare fees on loan offers—look for aid with low (or no) fees.
- Pay off your loans early to avoid paying more interest.
- Check out programs that cancel your loans or pay your tuition.
- Think about becoming a teacher or joining the military.

to $9,450 over two years to cancel loans or pay tuition. For more information, visit http://www.teachforamerica.org.

Serving in the military can cancel some of your loans, too. In fact, the Army National Guard offers up to $20,000 to pay back loans through its Student Loan Repayment Program. Visit http://www.1-800-Go-Guard.com for more information. The military also offers tuition assistance programs. Men and women serving in the U.S. Army, Navy, Marines, Coast Guard, and Air Force can have their tuition fully paid through the Armed Forces Tuition Assistance Program.

In 2007, Congress created the Public Service Loan Forgiveness Program to encourage graduates to choose long-term careers in public service. In the past, graduates with large student loan balances to repay may have gravitated away from these personally rewarding but often lower-paying careers. According to the rules of this program, individuals can have the balance of their eligible federal student loans forgiven after making 120 payments while working full-time in a public service organization. Since it takes borrowers about ten years to qualify, the first cancellations of loan balances will be granted in October 2017. For more information, go to http://www.federalstudentaid.ed.gov and search for "Loan Forgiveness for Public Service Employees."

Work-Study Programs

Work-study programs let you pay some of your college costs by working. They can also give you experience in career fields that you want to work in after college.

Federal Work-Study Program

The Federal Work-Study Program is need-based, so it depends on how much your family can pay for college. As a result, students from low-income families are more likely to get these jobs than students from high-income families. This program offers students jobs like lab assistants, writers/interviewers, library aides, designers, and food service employees. You can work on or off campus. While you work, you earn money for school.

The amount of work hours, the type of work, and the hourly pay depend on your job and financial situation. They also depend on the availability of jobs at your school. Your salary is

The National Commission for Cooperative Education (http://www.co-op.edu) provides information on programs that combine college studies with paid work experience in your intended field.

mostly paid by the federal government (about 75 percent), but also by your college (about 25 percent). The money you earn can reach, but not exceed, the amount of financial assistance you need. If you receive work-study as part of your financial aid package, contact your college's financial aid office to find a job. Some schools give you a job. Others post job listings for you to look through.

Cooperative Education Program

Like the Federal Work-Study Program, cooperative education programs, also called "co-ops," allow you to earn money for college while going to school. However, cooperative education programs are not need-based. Also, they typically allow you to do jobs that are relevant to your major or career goals.

Participating in a co-op program can affect how long it takes you to graduate. Usually, a student in a co-op program finishes a four-year course of study in five years. But during this time, you're getting job experience in the field in which you would like to work. Almost half the people in cooperative education programs work for the same employer after they graduate. In many cases, you can earn money for school and have a job once you graduate, without even looking! Not all colleges offer this program, so do the research. For more information, contact the National Commission for Cooperative Education (http://www.co-op.edu). On the Web site, you can download the organization's guide to the best co-op colleges and employers.

Myth: The sticker price is what I will pay for college.

Fact: Most students pay less than the sticker price for college. Some pay much less.

Myth: Every student attending the same college has the same out-of-pocket expenses.

Fact: The amount that a student pays out of pocket depends on many factors, including part-time or full-time status, state residency, financial aid packages, off-campus work, and housing choice.

Myth: I have to fill out the financial aid and scholarship forms by myself.

Fact: Guidance counselors, college financial aid officers, and online support will help you.

Myth: I have to fill out the Free Application for Federal Student Aid (FAFSA) in English.

Fact: The FAFSA can be filled out online or by mail in either English or Spanish.

Myth: There is no such thing as free money for college.

Fact: Scholarships and grants are free money. They are "gift aid" that doesn't have to be paid back.

Myth: I cannot apply for need-based aid.

Fact: Anyone can apply for need-based aid, but not everyone will receive it.

Chapter 5

Grants and Scholarships

Grants and scholarships are free money for college. The government, colleges, organizations, and companies give them out, and you don't have to pay them back. Grants and scholarships can be need-based or merit-based. Merit-based scholarships depend on your talents, background, interests, personal qualities, or life experiences. You can apply for as many grants and scholarships as you want.

Grants

The government and colleges usually give out grants. The largest government grant is the Federal Pell Grant. It is need-based. Millions of low-income families receive this grant each year. The amount you receive depends on whether you are a part-time or full-time student. Starting July 1, 2009, the largest amount awarded in a Federal Pell Grant increased to $5,350. The Federal Supplement Education Opportunity Grant, given by colleges, also provides money to families who need the most help to pay for college.

Need-based grants require you to fill out the FAFSA. In addition, state governments often give out grants to students living and attending colleges in the state.

Databases such as FastWeb (http://www.fastweb.com) help you find scholarships that match your interests, achievements, background, special needs, and future career.

Scholarships

It's important to know there are scholarships out there for everyone. You can get a scholarship for living in your state, getting good grades, being good in sports, growing up in a foster home, wanting to be a teacher, having learning disabilities, and many other reasons. There are more than 1.5 million scholarships available.

The best places to look for scholarships are online, in books, and in your own backyard. The largest database used to find scholarships is http://www.fastweb.com. To create a profile, you have to answer about twenty minutes' worth of questions. Then FastWeb matches you with possible scholarships, sends you e-mails with more matches, and helps you apply for scholarships online—all for free. A number of other Web sites, including the College Board's Scholarship Search (http://apps.collegeboard.com/cbseach_ss/welcome.jsp) and Scholarships.com, also provide information on scholarships.

Books with scholarships are found in your school library and your local public library. These books organize scholarships by categories, such as your home state, ethnic group, academic and career interests, and disabilities. They also provide information on money amounts, number of available scholarships, application

Talk to your parents, teachers, community and religious leaders, and guidance counselor about scholarship and grant opportunities.

deadlines, how to apply, and eligibility requirements (such as the requirement to be a freshman or sophomore).

Check the descriptions for specific requirements, such as having a minimum grade point average or going to a certain

There are more than 1.5 million available scholarships. Don't miss out because you did not apply.

school. If a scholarship is based on academic performance, your grades count. With school-specific scholarships, you have to go to the school that gives them out. However, portable merit scholarships can be used at any community college or four-year college.

Learning about local scholarships is one of the best ways to begin. Ask your school guidance counselor, teachers, religious leaders, community leaders, local business owners, and your parents' places of work about scholarship opportunities. Although many scholarships are given out by organizations and businesses, your local government can also give out scholarships. Check it out!

Who Are You?

Finding the right scholarship is all about knowing who you are. Try answering these questions to figure out which scholarship categories to concentrate on:

- What city or state do you live in?
- What is your ethnic background (for example, Caucasian, African American, Latino, or Asian)?
- Do you get good grades?
- Do you have a disability?
- What kinds of activities do you do (such as sports, clubs, or band)?
- Have you won any awards?
- Do you have a job?
- Have you done any volunteer work?
- What do you plan to study in college?

You can also receive scholarships depending on your family. Does your family qualify for financial aid? If the answer is yes, consider need-based scholarships. Did your grandparents or parents serve in the military? If they did, look at the military sections in the scholarship books. Does your family belong to a house of worship (like a church or synagogue) or a religious or cultural organization? These places may give out scholarships, too.

The Application Process

Applying for a scholarship begins with getting the application. In some cases, you may have to send a letter (with a self-addressed, stamped envelope) to request an application. Always follow the application's directions. Need-based scholarships also require you to fill out the FAFSA.

Scholarship applications may ask you for personal essays (usually about five hundred words each), a list of awards and extracurricular activities (like clubs, sports, or volunteer work), and one to three letters of recommendation. These items give you a chance to show the real you. They can also be used for your college

Avoid Scholarship Scams

Just as there are financial aid consulting scams, there are also scholarship scams. Avoid the following:

- Scholarship ads that use the word "guarantee" or promise "results, or your money back"
- Organizations or individuals that claim to have information that no one else has
- People who ask for your credit card information or money right away, especially to "hold a scholarship"

If you ever become the target of a scholarship scam, contact the Federal Trade Commission online, at http://www.ftc.gov, or by phone, at (877) 382-4357.

applications. If you're applying for an academic scholarship, you may need to provide a transcript (an official record of your grades) and copies of your test scores. Writing and art scholarships usually require writing samples or pictures of your artwork. Performing arts scholarships may require auditions.

Scholarship applications can involve an interview conducted over the phone or in person. During such an interview, you may be asked to describe yourself, list your strengths and weaknesses, name someone you admire, say why you want to go to college and what you would like to study, and reveal your college choices. To prepare for a scholarship interview, think about how you would answer these questions and practice delivering your answers.

When you receive a scholarship, it may be paid in full to you or the school. It can also be paid in smaller amounts by semesters or in another way. Some scholarships have an expiration date—for example, the scholarship may state, "You have up to twelve years after you graduate high school to use this scholarship." Others can be renewed. That is, you can receive another scholarship from the same organization for the next year. Make sure you understand the terms of your scholarships. A financial aid officer can explain them, and all organizations providing them have contact information.

Conclusion

You have the opportunity to make $1 million more in a lifetime than someone who only has a high school diploma. You have the chance to learn new skills, gain new life experiences, and get a good job. You have the chance to go to college.

Good choices can make college affordable for you. Community colleges cost less than four-year colleges, and a public college usually costs less than a private one. Financial aid can also fill the gap between what your dream college costs and what you can afford to pay.

More than half of American students receive financial aid to pay for college. This financial aid includes loans, grants and scholarships, and work-study programs. Government, colleges, businesses, and organizations give out billions of dollars in need-based and merit-based aid every year.

Everyone can apply for financial aid, but you must apply to get your share. Begin by researching your options early, such as the summer before your senior year. Try to fill out the FAFSA in January. And make sure you understand your financial aid offers.

College is your ticket to a better life. It is so important that President Barack Obama made it a goal for the United States to have the most college graduates in the world by 2020. This year, make college your goal, too.

Bachelor of Arts (B.A.) degree A type of undergraduate degree earned at a four-year college; also called a bachelor's degree.

college savings plan A plan that allows parents to save money to pay for their children's education while receiving tax-free benefits.

community college A two-year college located in one's community; it is often less expensive per year than a four-year college.

cost of attendance (COA) The total price of college, including direct and indirect costs.

direct costs The costs that are paid directly to the college, such as tuition and room and board.

expected family contribution (EFC) The amount of money a family is expected to pay for their children's college education.

financial aid Money given out by the government, colleges, businesses, and organizations to help students pay for college.

Free Application for Federal Student Aid (FAFSA) A form, available in English and Spanish, that is required to apply for need-based aid.

grant Financial aid that is awarded based on financial need or academic performance; it doesn't have to be paid back.

indirect costs The costs that are not directly paid to the college, such as transportation; also called variable costs.

inflation A rise in the general price level of goods and services.

interest rate The cost of borrowing money, expressed as a percentage of the loan amount.

Loan Borrowed money. The borrower promises to pay it back according to certain conditions.

Loan default Failure to repay a loan.

Loan forgiveness Canceling, or forgiving, part of a loan.

Master of Arts (M.A.) degree A type of graduate degree earned at a four-year college; also called a master's degree.

merit-based aid Financial aid that depends on a talent, background, interest, personal quality, or life experience.

need-based aid Financial aid that depends on expected family contribution.

private college A college that doesn't receive funding mainly from the state government. It is privately funded.

public college A college that is mainly funded by the state government.

room and board The cost of living in a dormitory room, with a meal plan; it can also include electricity, phone, and Internet access.

scholarship Gift aid that can be merit-based or need-based; it doesn't have to be paid back.

Student Aid Report (SAR) Summary of the FAFSA that includes the expected family contribution.

tax credit A tax break that helps parents pay for their children's education, such as the Hope Scholarship Tax Credit.

tuition The cost of attending college classes.

Alliance for Young Artists & Writers
The Scholastic Art and Writing Awards
557 Broadway
New York, NY 10012
(212) 343-6100
Web site: http://www.scholastic.com/artandwriting
This program gives more than nine hundred awards, including a
$20,000 art award and a $10,000 writing award. Writing or
art/graphic samples are required.

Children's Scholarship Fund
8 West 38th Street, 9th Floor
New York, NY 10018
(212) 515-7100
Web site: http://www.scholarshipfund.org
This organization provides scholarships for low-income families.
Its Web site gives information on scholarships that are
available in each state.

Coca-Cola Scholars Foundation
P.O. Box 442 (For four-year awards for seniors)
P.O. Box 1615 (For two-year college scholarships)
Atlanta, GA 30301
Web site: http://www.coca-colascholars.org
This foundation provides fifty scholarships of $20,000 each and
two hundred scholarships of $4,000 each to students every
year. Grades, work experience, and school/volunteer activi-
ties are considered.

College Board
45 Columbus Avenue

New York, NY 10023-6917
(866) 630-9305; International: (212) 520-8570
Web site: http://www.collegeboard.com
This organization provides information on standardized exams
like the SATs, finding and applying to colleges, college
costs, and financial aid opportunities. It also has information
for students with disabilities.

National Association of Student Financial Aid
Administrators (NASFAA)
1101 Connecticut Avenue NW, Suite 1100
Washington, DC 20036-4303
(202) 785-0453
Web site: http://www.nasfaa.org
The "Parents & Students" section on the NASFAA Web site
provides information on completing the FAFSA and finding
scholarships and loan forgiveness programs. It also has a
link to the FAFSA in both English and Spanish.

National Commission for Cooperative Education
360 Huntington Avenue, 384 CP
Boston, MA 02115
(617) 373-3770
Web site: http://www.co-op.edu
This organization provides an application for the National
Co-op Scholarship Program. Its Web site lists participating
colleges with their scholarship money amounts.

National Sciences and Engineering Research
Council of Canada
350 Albert Street

Ottawa, ON K1A 1H5
Canada
(613) 995-4273
Web site: http://www.nserc-crsng.gc.ca
This council gives out scholarships and grants to Canadian
    citizens in various areas of study.

U.S. Department of Education
400 Maryland Avenue SW
Washington, DC 20202
(800) USA-LEARN (1-800-872-5327)
Web site: http://www.ed.gov/index.jhtml
The Web site for this federal government department explains
    why you should go to college and how to pay for it. It also
    gives useful information on available loans, making loan
    payments, and loan defaults.

Web Sites

Due to the changing nature of Internet links, Rosen Publishing
has developed an online list of Web sites related to the subject
of this book. This site is updated regularly. Please use this link
to access this list:

http://www.rosenlinks.com/col/pfc

For Further Reading

Cassidy, Daniel J. *The Scholarship Book: The Complete Guide to Private-Sector Scholarships, Fellowships, Grants, and Loans for the Undergraduate*. New York, NY: Prentice Hall Press, 2008.

Chany, Kalman A., and Geoff Martz. *Paying for College Without Going Broke: 2010 Edition*. New York, NY: Random House/Princeton Review, 2009.

College Board. *College Handbook 2009*. New York, NY: The College Board, 2008.

College Board. *Getting Financial Aid 2009*. New York, NY: The College Board, 2008.

College Board. *Scholarship Handbook 2009*. New York, NY: The College Board, 2008.

Kaplan, Ben. *How to Go to College Almost for Free*. New York, NY: HarperCollins, 2002.

Kravets, Marybeth, and Imy F. Wax. *The K & W Guide to Colleges for Students with Learning Disabilities or Attention Deficit/Hyperactivity Disorder*. New York, NY: Princeton Review, 2007.

Schlachter, Gail Ann, and R. David Weber. *Directory of Financial Aid for Women 2007–2009*. El Dorado Hills, CA: Reference Service Press, 2007.

Schlachter, Gail Ann, and R. David Weber. *Financial Aid for African Americans, 2008–2010*. El Dorado Hills, CA: Reference Service Press, 2008.

Schlachter, Gail Ann, and R. David Weber. *Financial Aid for Asian Americans, 2008–2010*. El Dorado Hills, CA: Reference Service Press, 2008.

Schlachter, Gail Ann, and R. David Weber. *Financial Aid for the Disabled and Their Families, 2008–2010*. El Dorado Hills, CA: Reference Service Press, 2008.

Schlachter, Gail Ann, and R. David Weber. *Financial Aid for Hispanic Americans, 2008–2010*. El Dorado Hills, CA: Reference Service Press, 2008.

Schlachter, Gail Ann, and R. David Weber. *Financial Aid for Native Americans, 2008–2010*. El Dorado Hills, CA: Reference Service Press, 2008.

Schlachter, Gail Ann, and R. David Weber. *Financial Aid for Veterans, Military Personnel, and Their Dependents, 2008–2010*. El Dorado Hills, CA: Reference Service Press, 2008.

Schlachter, Gail Ann, and R. David Weber. *Kaplan Scholarships 2009*. New York, NY: Kaplan Publishing, 2008.

Tanabe, Gen, and Kelly Tanabe. *The Ultimate Scholarship Book, 2009*. Belmont, CA: SuperCollege LLC, 2008.

U.S. News & World Report. *Ultimate College Guide*. Naperville, IL: Sourcebooks, Inc., 2008.

Bibliography

Anderson, Trent, and Seppy Basili. *Paying for College: Lowering the Cost of Higher Education*. New York, NY: Kaplan Publishing, 2007.

Clark, Kim. "Financial Aid Applications Rise by 10 Percent." *U.S. News & World Report*, January 13, 2009. Retrieved February 2009 (http://www.usnews.com/articles/education/2009/01/13/financial-aid-applications-rise-by-10-percent.html).

College Board. "2008–09 College Prices," "How the Borrowing Process Works," and "Scholarships & Aid." CollegeBoard.com. Retrieved February 2009 (http://www.collegeboard.com/student/pay/add-it-up/4494.html).

FAFSA: Free Application for Federal Student Aid. "Home Page." 2009. Retrieved February 2009 (www.fafsa.ed.gov).

FinAid. "Student Loans." FinAid.org. Retrieved February 2009 (http://www.finaid.org/loans).

Hechinger, John, and Craig Karmin. "Harvard Hit by Loss as Crisis Spreads to Colleges." *Wall Street Journal*, December 4, 2008. Retrieved February 2009 (http://online.wsj.com/article/SB122832139322576023.html).

Hechinger, John, Laura Meckler, and Robert Tomsho. "Experts Wonder How Education Goals Will Be Met." *Wall Street Journal*, February 26, 2009. Retrieved March 2009 (http://online.wsj.com/article/SB123561145508077643.html).

Kantrowitz, Barbara. "Now Take a Deep Breath." Kaplan/*Newsweek*'s *How to Get Into College 2009*, Summer 2009, pp. 6–9.

Kaplan, Ben. *The Scholarship Scouting Report*. New York, NY: Harper Collins, 2003.

Peterson's. *Paying for College*. Lawrenceville, NJ: Peterson's, 2008.

Rye, David. *The Complete Idiot's Guide to Financial Aid for College*. New York, NY: Penguin Group, 2008.

Sallie Mae. "Home Page." SallieMae.com. Retrieved February 2009 (http:/www.salliemae.com).

Tanabe, Gen, and Kelly Tanabe. *The Ultimate Scholarship Book, 2009*. Belmont CA: SuperCollege LLC, 2008.

Tomsho, Robert. "For College-Bound, New Barriers to Entry." *Wall Street Journal*, December 3, 2008. Retrieved February 2009 (http://online.wsj.com/article/SB122826544902474353.html).

U.S. Bureau of Labor Statistics. "College Enrollment and Work Activity of 2007 High School Graduates." April 25, 2008. Retrieved February 2009 (http://www.bls.gov/news.release/hsgec.nr0.htm).

Index

About the Author

Barbara Gottfried Hollander has a B.A. degree in economics from the University of Michigan and an M.A. degree in economics from New York University, specializing in statistics and econometrics. She is the author of *Managing Money* and *Raising Money*, and is the economics and education editor of the *2009 World Almanac and Book of Facts*. Hollander has designed, written, and assessed courses in finance, marketing, accounting, mathematics, and economics and the environment for the Knowledge Learning Corporation and has written standardized testing material for the Educational Testing Service and New Leaders for New Schools. She also promotes literacy in special needs schools through her involvement with the Literacy Connections Committee. Hollander lives in New Jersey with her husband and their three children.

Photo Credits

Cover, p. 1 © www.istockphoto.com/René Mansi; p. 4 Yellow Dog Productions/Lifesize/Getty Images; pp. 10, 34, 51 Shutterstock.com; pp. 12–13 James Woodson/Digital Vision/Getty Images; pp. 14–15, 25, 41, 49, 55, 65, 66 © www.istockphoto.com/Robert Dant; pp. 17, 23, 29 © AP Images; p. 19 Ryan McVay/Digital Vision/Getty Images; p. 20 Darren McCollester/Getty Images; p. 27 © www.istockphoto.com/Sean Locke; p. 33 © St. Petersburg Times/ZUMA Press; p. 36 © David Young-Wolff/PhotoEdit; pp. 38–39, 62–63 © James Marshall/The Image Works; p. 48 Loren Santow/Stone/Getty Images; pp. 52–53 © Flores, Elizabeth/Star Tribune/ZUMA Press; p. 64 John Guistina/Photodisc/Getty Images.

Designer: Nicole Russo; Editor: Andrea Sclarow; Photo Researcher: Cindy Reiman

Y 378.3809 HOLLANDER
Hollander, Barbara,
Paying for college :
  practical, creative
  strategies

RO119518883   EAST_A

EAST ATLANTA
Atlanta-Fulton Public Library